Heartbreak With Fries, Please

A poetry book of Je Ne Sais Quoi

Dr. Ishana Ghosh

BookLeaf Publishing
India | USA | UK

Made with ❤ on the BookLeaf Publishing Platform
www.bookleafpub.in
www.bookleafpub.com

Dedication

Someone once told me,
"Love keeps us kind, even when we are let down."

This book is for anyone who has ever dared to love with kindness.

Preface

Hi You,

Hope you are doing well.
Here is a brief insight into this book.

I started writing poetry back in 2010, inspired by someone very important to me and I have not stopped since.
The earliest piece in this book dates back to the beginning of 2019. Back then I had just started my third year of Medical College and would often take to my phone's notes app, attempting to write down my thoughts, as that is how I majorly process my emotions. There is something cathartic about reading the words born out of my own volition, back to myself, that helps me clearly navigate through the multifaceted layering of emotional cognition, at least the part of it that is comprehensible.
This book is a compilation of poems composed over years ranging from then to now, some written within a few minutes and never visited again, some written and re-written, some still a work in progress.

The poems seamlessly interconnect, allowing you to navigate them in any direction for your pleasure.

I hope you get something out of this.

I did.

Acknowledgements

"Strangers passing in the street
By chance two separate glances meet
And I am you and what I see is me
And do I take you by the hand
And lead you through the land
And help me understand the best I can"- *Pink Floyd*

1. Resting Eclipse

I wrote this piece on a windy night and something about the way in which my bedroom curtains were swaying in the wind only intensified the solitude of that particularly lonely night. I was pining for someone and had no way to let them know and so...

It's this bed

I've been laying in
for months now, at an end.
This night sees no end.

And yet somehow
I've been taught to pretend
that the dawn marks the end
of this endless night,

It doesn't.

I don't wake up with the sun,
I don't even sleep,
I'm suspended in an eclipse
of the heart,
where day and night know no meaning,
for all meaning is lost
but what is found is a sense,
born of deprivation.
Raging, almost feeding
this great eclipse,
consuming all that makes sense,
till what is left behind is incomprehensible.

And I'm suspended furthermore.

Aching, I long to *rest* my back
on this bed of *love.*
Aching for a deep slumber
to end this endless night
and drive me into the greatest of all nights,
where meaning has no meaning
and all is lost where it is found.

Aching for an eclipse
of the mind and not my heart.

For let my heart break.
Let it keep breaking,
till breaking has lost all meaning,
and my heart has lost all hope,
and my mind has lost all sense of self.

Till my mind knows not my heart,
and my heart knows no hurt,

and I,
I will know
neither of them.

And I'll know,
that I'm aching no more.

2. To Be Young And In Love

There is a lake in Kolkata which I frequented with someone who meant a lot to me and even though we went there together maybe 3 or 4 times, we had declared a spot for ourselves by the edge of the lake where we would sit, our legs dangling over the water beneath. We exchanged many conversations at this spot, some of which have greatly influenced many pieces in this book. One of them is this piece.
I could never go back to that spot and feel what I had felt with him. I tried.

I've aged a lifetime

since we first met.
Closing in on 3 years
we're almost ashore,
separated by a *Pacific* of pain in between.
Maybe someday,
we'll tell each other everything.

Sitting two steps away
from our spot.
Fighting the urge to gravitate
to all that's left behind.
Two kids *riding the wave,*
they're looking for an escape,
prisoners of the mind.
"Can I kiss you?"
Something comes alive.

"Is this love?"
What if it is, she says.

What if it's not.

Took me 3 years to give it a thought.

So I drift away, beyond what I can see.
I figured out how to flow
while the water stands still.
Your *mind* always gave me a *thrill.*
Inculcated a little bit of you in me.
I'll hold onto it,
so for a moment I can feel you in me.

If even for a moment I can feel you,

then that is all I need.

Standing at our spot,
I almost forgot,
how it feels to be loved,
and to love.
Sensing a memory floating around here somewhere.
I'm tempted to taste it,
it might reverse my ageing.

But I let it go.
Walking past, I leave the kids alone.
They're so indifferent to me.
Free from the what if and what could be,

Unafraid of undying *uncertainty.*

Their love, an eclipse resting in time,
so I let it be.

3. Mind

Another piece of yearning for unrequited love. Here I am trying to sell myself the narrative that I am moving on, but really it would be years before that happens. This here, is an attempt at forgetting someone.

On afternoons like this,

the sunlight hits
old lost corners of my mind,
and I'm, oh, but a slave to *time*.

I'm approaching you
in forsaken avenues,
to let go, to not confine
these shadows of You and I.

It's lost, but not *forgotten,*
the sentiments remain.
Though I fear of losing you

on afternoons like today.

I met myself wounded, tired,
hands bloodied with a crime.
It took a while to ease in,
but now I'm all mine.

To let go, to hold on,
I could never decide.
But somewhere down the line,
I forgot to even try.

Wearing your T-shirt
in a cold shower on a sultry day,
hearing myself say things I never got to say.
Would you hear them, if I asked you to stay?

I'm not scared of what I've become.
Settled into my grief, I've come *undone*
Did I *love* you then? Back when we were *young*,
Or has it all been, a melody unsung?

Lost but not forgotten
corners of time
lay me down, they help define
this painstaking guilt trip we both abide by.

But now I must face the truth.
Have I forgotten you?
Surgically excised, when did I
forget you?
I can't remember.
Do you not remember me too?

Dust settles on these moments
when I wonder,
If I ever got to know your mind.

4. Time : An Endless Knot

The Endless Knot is a sacred Buddhist Symbol depicting the endless nature of love and life. There was a book with this symbol made on it that me and my person had bought from a small bookstore and the book was where I had started writing all my poems.
This piece is a commemoration of the love we had for each other. It is an unending piece as the ending is the same as the beginning.

An *Endless* Knot

taking us through
Space and Time.
I'm not yours,
You aren't mine,
yet a sweet subside
we find ourselves in,
descending and ascending
through paths divine.

Ghosts playing
the forgotten keys
at a Victorian lodge,
bring us to a standstill.
In the ballroom,
You and I so still.
And in the thrill of it all,
our hands interlock,
we begin to sing along.

Dim lights, heavy bass drops,
we share a Marlboro.
High on Apple Cinnamon,
the gin, the tonic,
sipping whiskey and rum,
we begin to come *undone*.
Clinking beer bottles,
foaming cappuccino,
the air is alcoholic.

Old lovers lost in time
meet once again.
I see why You love her,
I see through Your ache.
She is pretty, she is kind,
bold and perky and sublime.

But You're more than she could ever take.
Let me show You how to heal Your heartbreak.

Ruffled sheets,
candles flickering eerily,
I guide you into me.
You know the way through,
You know the warmth within,
January subzero *temperature burning up,*
Baby we are hotter than the sun.
You realize I could be the one.

Soul numbing hunger
brings us to our knees.
Blood sugar spikes,
but the hunger
can't be satisfied.
Imagination running wild,
turning me on with your *mind.*

Your songs make me cry.
Their beauty,
puts the Moon Peak to shame.
Listening to Jane, the *hills* witness our
lovemaking,
every night.
A hard surrender to sleep,

we wake up to golden rays.

Strolling through decades old
prayer bars,
onlookers wonder
how are we so much in love.
They wish us well
through shared conversations
and we laugh along,
playing the part of *kids in love.*

Little do we know,
that we aren't kids anymore,
like we were two and a half years before.
And I see Your sins for all the substance they hold.
You look into my eyes, and see a story being told.
It goes like this,
I might not be yours, You might not be mine,
but we are entangled in Space and Time,
yet to traverse so many paths divine.

A year can change a lot,
hollows and hex,
high altitude treks,
they are small blots
in the larger scheme of things.
We make our own plot,

we make our dreams come true,
we heal each other though our art,
which heals the world through and through.
Birth, death, rebirth
that's all we got.

It's all a dance,
to the *tune* of God,
the only one there ever was.

We are,
An *Endless* Knot
taking us through
Space and Time.
I'm not yours,
You aren't mine,
yet a sweet subside
we find ourselves in,
descending and ascending
through paths divine.

(continues on loop for it’s an Endless Knot)

5. Cold January

This piece is about a great personal tragedy that engulfed me a few years ago.

When you feel you need your lover

to be your friend just for a while,
and you know you're wrong for needing
a friend, who doesn't even know that you want to die.
When all you need is all you have,
and all you have is fading away,
all of you wants to make it through,
but not even a bit of you can bear another day.

When your heart's so broken,
you don't even know
how to give yourself the love you have.
When you're dead,
you're only dead.

not even a memory someone once had.

Where to go to lose it all?
Then come back to lose some more.
When all the hurt you could have borne,
is too much hurt and now you want more.

Your mind is crushed, you lost yourself,
you lost the fight, you lost the will
you lost the love, you lost the friend,
where will you go to find an end?

Cause when you're dead,
you're only dead.
But is that the end of you?
How can it be, when there is no end
to this love you need to help you through.
Please tell me then, what do I do?
For my lover is not a friend.
Even I don't love myself tonight.

Even I would break my heart in two.

Who then, will save me now,
from the shit that comes with another sunrise?
When I've left myself lying dead and loveless,
like the ruins of a motherless *child.*

And I've killed your trust, I know.
But will I ever know what I've done?
When all of me has been bled out,
only memories remain of this horror show
which we call life, and I live it well.
I work, I drive, I buy groceries too.
I cook, I eat, I nurture my plants,
as if I'm not a killer anymore.

But I swear to you, I could kill someone,
and my hands would shake a little less
than anyone else who hasn't seen
their own love bleed out of themselves.

All I need is all I've given away,
now there is nothing left for me.
Time stands still, my mind might make it to 83.
But all of me died this January.

6. Child

This piece is about a young girl who is trying to navigate through the obstacles that life keeps throwing her way. It's about resilience and also about defeat.

This one is dedicated to all the young girls out there, who are just trying to survive.

There's a little girl I see

standing right next to me,
reaching out for a hand to hold,
my offer she won't receive.
Running through an *endless* maze
of being alive and not being alright.
Running out of places where she
could *rest* for an eternity.
She smiles and says, "I'll be fine,
this is my time, I'll make it mine.
If time refuses to hold my *hand*,

that's just another *wave I'll have to ride.*"

She will become certainly,
an endless maze of uncertainty.
And when she does, I hope she'll find,
she's been the wave all this time.
And *nothing* that she might need,
will ever be,
beyond her reach.

I've seen her face out in the dark,
searching for her missing art,
longing for a mother's love
and a father's lonely broken heart.
She's seen it all, she's just a child.
She's been it all, she's turning wild.
With hopes and dreams that sing a song
of a sweeter past and bruises mild.
And she knows the song all too well
to ever try and sing along,
yet, she draws a heavy breath,
letting out a *tune* of a lifetime.

Sing along, you know it too,
you know the worth you've had to prove.
Remember the bruises you've had to bear,
from innocent hands that you have held.

And maybe then your hand she'll hold
and guide you in. You'll guide her through
this endless maze of *uncertainty.*
Now she has the help she needs.

She's standing here for me to see,
that this little girl is all I need.
Yet I don't know where she will go
when the song is over,
and your hand turns *cold.*

7. Nothing At All

This piece is dystopian and ethereal. One of my more abstract works.

When the sun falls

You see it burn away
Come up again someday
And you fade away

And mother, Susan
Is calling out *your name*

Flashes
Are going by, you realize that everything
Is nothing but a lie

And what is left are pieces of tomorrowland
And all that came, yesterday.

Everything
Everyone
All the things, left to learn
Are coming in
They'll drown your *skin*
So run along
To nowhere
And no one.

When the winds blow
You see them blow away
Sorrows and misery
And you fade away

And brother, *Steven*
Is screaming out somewhere.

Echoes
Are flying high, you realize that every time
He cries *child,* it's your name.

And what is left are moments of togetherness
And nothing is the same.

River comes to the sea,
Who is to say it's not you and me.

If you think about it, everything just comes around to....
A stop.

Everything
Everyone
All the things, left to learn
And all the things left to do
Will never come,
To anyone,
Ever.

8. Steven // Lullabies

This piece is about Steven Wilson, one of my music heroes and how I felt upon reading his book 'Limited Edition Of One'.
It is also about my love for someone who covered many of Porcupine Trees's songs.

I sound British.

My voice, of a man's
who has given me much to think about,
if not more to understand.

I slipped in and out of him
for the better half of a minute.
He was the voice inside my head.
Should it be disconcerting
that the realization wasn't?
Should I fall asleep in the *darkest* dread?

I read about a dream he had
when he was six or seven.
It's the only highlighted text
you'll find in my Limited Edition Of One.

And all I could think about
was, how to share
what I'd just read,
with you.
For I believe you'd get him
exactly the way I do.

You introduced me to his music,
a door into his mind.
How absurd should it be,
that I would find you,
repeatedly,
in most of his absurdities.

I'd never heard Blackest Eyes,
until I heard of it through you.
Your brilliant performance of it,
that I missed,
so that now I can't hear the song
and not remember you. All of you.

Your rendition of Happy Returns. Brilliant.

Now I'll turn the page,
onto another chapter.
As will you.
Nothing remains of us.

I know I've lost the right to wish
that upon reading his book, in his words somewhere,
you'll meet me there.
The sentiment you'll find,
might take you *back in time,*
to when I was *singing* along with you
to lullabies and Lazarus.

9. Darkest Nights

Some pieces leave you bare and broken once you are done with them. This is one of them.

I wonder where you are on the darkest nights

Of my life
I wonder if you still fall asleep
To my lullabies
That I wrote for you with love
Though it never was enough
Oh I *sing* them to myself now
Knowing that you'll never come
Around
Around

I wonder where you are when the streets
Shimmer in lights
And if you still remember how I'd sing

Into the night
Oh I'd sing to you with love
But it never was enough
I just stare into the sky now
Knowing that you'll never come
Around
Around

Would you please forgive me
If I say
I don't need love
I don't need love
Would you please forgive me
If I *call your name*

Would you please forgive me
If I say
I don't need your love
I don't need your love
Would you please forgive me
If I cry in pain

Why am I in pain?
Would you hear me then?
Would you hear me then?
Would you hear me then?
Say you'll hear me then

Just say you'll come
Around
Around

I wonder where you are on the darkest nights
Of my life
I wonder if you still fall asleep
To my *lullabies*

10. Why

Another such piece of paramount sadness.

You said you'd never go away
But here I am all alone
You said you would always be my friend
But there's no *one calling me on the phone*

And every time I think about you
All I see are pretty *lies*
And every time I *cry*
There are no *tears* in my eyes

So why
Did you go away
Why

I said I'll give you everything
As long as I have my *skin and my bones*

I said you'd never sleep alone
I'd guide you into my *home*

And then you walked away from everything
That we had going on
And even then I just
Hold on

Oh why
Did you go away
Why

Everything about us
Is killing me
Everything that kept me alive
Everything about us
Is killing me
Everything, on this *dark night*

Everything about us
Is killing me
I need you here by my side

So why did you have to go
When all I need is you
Why did you have to go
When all I need is you

Why

You said you'd never go away
But here I am all alone
You said you would always be my friend
There's no one calling me on the phone

11. Cry For Release

This is one of my latest works, something I wrote few days before finalizing this book, making me realize that relapse into heartbreak and grief is a part of the process and is progress in it's own way.

I cried when I saw *your name.*

It's like you exist again
outside of my suppression,
a *denial* of my obsession.
I'm sorry for the anxiety,
I'll never forgive myself.
There's guilt in each gap,
like pressure built in a spinal tap,

and seeing your name
felt like a sweet release
of the guilt, the pressure, the spinal fluid.
The Anaesthesia is in my *brain,*

it's making me hallucinate.
I feel the beginning of forgiveness
by you,
or is it just the propofol?
In reality, it doesn't exist *at all.*

But your name shines on
through the screen, burning into my eyes,
my mind, my *soul*, my heart, my memory, *flashes* of you
holding me.
I'm being cut open by your memory,
or is it just this surgery, that's cutting into me ?
I don't know.
I'm stuck in a limbo
of an unconscious subconscious decree.
Am I waking up? The Anaesthesia is fading.
But my *guts* are still open,
should I scream?
Why am I hallucinating?
Are you really beginning to forgive me?
No, it's just a dream.
An awakening,

that your name
will never be what it was to me. I'll cry and re-live the
memory.
I'll let it cut into me.

I’m waking up
in the middle of this surgery,
a sweet release from this existence,
there's no forgiveness for me.

12. Guts

I've met you many times in my mind,

I've said everything in every way I wanted to say,
sometimes all at once, sometimes none *at all,*
each time it felt the same,
that *familiar* pang of pain
gut wrenching, head hurting,
mind numbing disdain.
No matter what I say, no matter how,
it never leaves me feeling better
than how I *feel* now.
And how I feel, you wouldn't want to know,
or maybe you would, maybe you hate me so?
I've tried to forgive you, tried to forgive myself,
tried to let it all go, oh how I fail.
It's like I inhale all the guilt, both of ours,
and never do I let myself exhale.
I *cry* and I cry, I cry for you and me.
I cry for us, for the people we used to be

to each other, to ourselves, to our friends, to 'our' friends;
Long gone, they've chosen sides, two ends of the *Pacific,*
You and I.

My anger defies me, so does regret,
I can never seem to find them on trying nights.
I never understood how you do it.
I rage against not you, but the years we've lost,
they are never to return at any cost.
They've added to the entropy of this ever expanding chaos
within which we could have built a pocket of endurance.
But now, the effort seems imaginary, meaningless, foregone.
And the memories of our love lost to the chaos of our lives.
I see you for not just the hate, but how much you love in spite of it.
And I can't unsee you in this *light,*
it colours your face in a way I cannot recognize.

Shadows under your eyes dancing beneath
a teary sky of stars, starry sky of *tears.*
I can't unsee your fears.
They stem from you and drain into me, drain me.
No, I can't be what you need me to be.

I lost myself to you,
that's when I lost you too.
I'm trying to remember who was I to me.

13. Feel My Skin

This piece is an attempt to find a place of belonging.

I don't want to die

but I've never been alive,
the warmth in my *guts*
doesn't feel like it's mine.

Dreaming on borrowed time,
you wake me up too soon,
though your kiss is real,
it fails to make me feel,

what life could have been
for all of us today,
if we could just arrange
for another chance to play.

And the deeper I sink,

the faster we disappear.
You see me no more,
nothing left to fear.

Strip down this façade,
it's *burning you up* dear.
Your skin is on fire,
your cries I cannot hear.

What it all means,
for all of us today,
is that we have got to arrange
for another chance to play.

I don't want to die,
I just want to *arrive,*
to a *home* in my skin
and make it feel like it's mine.

14. Arrive

This piece was written on an airplane ride, just when I was beginning to develop flight anxiety.

Flying through thin air,
weightless yet heavy,
can we ever *rise* above?

The *light* glaring into my eyes,
I can see for miles and miles,
any moment I can bite the dust.

Clouds shaped like my insecurities,
it all seems *familiar* to me,
somewhat *forgotten*,
but mostly ignored.
I soar through the sky
in one piece, yet I'm torn.
Will I ever overcome?

Breathe into me
an air of hostility.
Feel my skin, show me the secrets of being *out of body.*
Don't need no pressure control,
some *temperature* malfunction,
to feed my *soul.*

Will I survive the fall?
I need to know.
Break open this window.

Take control of all that
which doesn't belong to me.
But who am I to set you free?

Sky, a strange shade of blue,
seems to me it's all new,
somewhat imagined,
but mostly false imagery.
I'm moving in time
in one piece, yet I'm infinite.

Will I ever arrive?

15. Out Of Body

This piece is inspired by 'Butoh Dance", a ritual wherein body movements are used as a means to rid the body of negative energy and embody death and morbidity in order to conquer them.

I feel the blood in my *brain,*
gushing through my tiny vein.
Shadows on my ceiling announce
a hemorrhage setting in,
there's no way out.

So I rush out of my body,
will stay away for tonight.
And when the shadows disappear,
my eyes will open to the morning *light.*
I'll be in my *skin* again
and I'll cry in pain,

feel the hemorrhage setting in,
as the blood floods my brain.

It'll go on for a while,
dancing of the spirits.
Their shadows paint my walls.
I tell myself I'm trapped in it,
this body that I grew up in,
but now I've outgrown it,
now I must leave every night
so I don't die in it.

And yet when I return,
drawing me in, the morning sun,
my head, it never stops spinning,
guess the hemorrhage is winning.

So I fight and I fight,
but can't escape the morning light,
this night, it seems, is paralyzed.

So I dance with the shadows every night
as I pray for them to *arrive* and I say,

"I feel a throbbing in my vein,
the blood is rotting my tiny brain,
let me stay out, not just for the night,

but even when my eyes see light.
And maybe soon I'll stop this dance,
take a breath and *rest* in peace,
I've fought my battle, I think I've won,
or maybe it was never meant to be."

16. Sleep Paralysis

This piece is inspired by someone who told me that they have experienced sleep paralysis and so I tried to put myself in their shoes, so as to feel how they must feel when they are in the eye of the storm.

I'm so wide awake

it's killing me inside,
my mind, it whispers
"Sleep is just *death* being shy."
And though I'm awake,
my *body* won't *rise.*
This night, it seems,
is paralyzed.

Let's dream of *green fields,*
where every breathe lasts,
the ground where we lie,
sings of it's past,

of hopes buried deep
within the bodies cold,
now fodder for the *grass*
where you hold me close,

and sing of a future
which we do not hold
and sing for this moment,
that exists no more.

You are wide awake
with dreams in your eyes,
that guide me far beyond
the drape of your *lies.*
They say you are content
and doing just fine,
when all you want
is to b*reak* through this *night.*

Into the black sky,
into the black hole,
into the black sea,
right through your heavy soul.

Let it float and unburden
the weights of our dreams,
while we sing ourselves,

sing ourselves to sleep

with a song of a future
that we do not hold,
as we die in this moment,
that exists no more.

17. Night Cage

This piece is an attempt to break free from the shackles of one's own mind.

And the *hills* cried,

shredding up the mist
as I come into myself,
leaving behind a *denial,*
a burial, a birth, that exists
in my mind's eye.

Won't you lift me up?
Hope you have the key
to escape this cage,
this cage that is me.

I'm in the wind,
the river flows in me,
pine roots grow deep

in chaotic symmetry.
I am alive, as are they,
but it's still a cage,
in this we cannot stay.

And the *moon* moaned
through the *sleepy* night,
we are alone on this ride.
Stars crystallize
this gloomy *grey sky,*
as we tremble on, you and I.

Won't you hold my *hand?*
Hope you have the sight
to guide me in the dark,
help me break out right.

I'm in the snow,
the sun cuts through me,
birds sing of sweet sorrow
in perfect harmony.
I am dying, as are they
within this cage.
We must fly away.

So come on honey,
let's run

into the woods
and never return.

I'll set you free,
as you come into me.

18. Hills : A Celestial Definition

This piece tries to capture the ravenous feeling that rests in the hills.

Faint stormy thoughts

fog up the *hills*,
pines cut through
the walls we instill.

Are these *clouds,* we force
upon our innocence,
that glide up the slopes
of self constructed reference?
Or are they mists of the past,
laden with *echoes,*
bouncing off lush
green fields of foes?
It's all but a point

in space, in time.
We exist, as we cease to,
nothing you can define.

Then comes the rain.
Drenched in introspection,
you pace back and forth,
till you're down with dejection.
The mind is wet,
intentions cold and *blue,*
I feel you feeling alive,
your art a numbing hue,

of all that I fear
and all that I crave,
sensory deprivation; you have me
in a hypnotic *haze.*
Silver shimmer
penetrating our pores,
our star dust atoms collide
as the *moon* excites our cores.
It can't be just a point,
we transcend *space and time,*
celestial *shadows,*
fly me through your mind,
we exist, yet we cease to.
Let's rage against this *cage tonight.*

19. Blue Tune

This piece is an ode to the moon and how it influences us in ways beyond comprehension.

The city is dark,
deeper than our dreams,
street lights shining *bright,*
guiding passers-by,
putting to shame
the dimly lit stars
of this night sky.

Neon bulbs flicker,
study lamps quiver,
lonely souls hustle on,
hoping to make it through
this night so demanding
yet strangely comforting,
as they embrace their youth.

Slow down or speed along,
turn in and dream on,
it's all true,
we are powered by the *moon.*

There ain't no doubt,
we can't stop dancing to a primal *tune.*

Celestial light kindles
through glass stained windows,
adding colour to black and white homes.

On and off goes a bulb
in a distant memory of you,
And it's all *blue.*
And it's all *blue.*

Some stumble, some fall,
some seem to have it all,
but then we don't move
to our own accord.

You know it's true,
we belong on the moon.
There we will *dance*
to our primal tune.

20. Full Moon In Scorpio

This piece a declaration of my love for the moon.

Missed the full *moon*

by a night,
but her *shine*, still mighty *bright.*
Layers upon layers in between us,
her touch, electrifying.
And I'm hooked.

Jaw dropping pearly white,
she reveals herself
ever so slightly.
The clouds, tempting me
to tear them apart,
I just want to feel her light.

It's a lonely night,
just me and her

and a beauty she is,
but she is more than that.
She's the calm in the wind,
she's the high tide,
she's the rustle in the leaves,
she's the midnight *sun,*
she's the love that comes *undone.*

Bathed in her company,
in love with the silence that prevails.
I long to take in that burst of light,
it's so gentle, it doesn't belong here.
Guilty pleasures as I take what's not mine
and I gaze, I gaze, I gaze,
I try to look away, I fail.
I can't believe what's in my sight.
I can't believe how relaxed I feel.
I don't belong here.

Slow *dancing* into this night,
wild blue tunes in my sight.
I give into a soft current
it's flowing through me,
as I set my worries aside.
The leaves, the wind, the sun,
a witness to this love affair.
I'm hers and *she's mine,*

at least for tonight.

And maybe she'll heal
the craters I've suppressed
over and over and over again.
Endless tears I've cried on endless nights,
yet tonight, she's in my sight,
and I feel alright.

It's been a while,

and I wish this night was
more than just a night.

21. Shine

This piece is about a shooting star I saw a few years ago and how in an instant, it left me with an everlasting feeling of gratefulness, for in that instance I was happy to be alive.

I left on a *shooting star*
that took my breath away.
She took me to the valley below,
in the dark of the *hills*, in the rain.

We touched for a moment,
and the moment was gone,
gone beyond my wildest dreams,
beyond the *full moon,* beyond the snow, beyond the river,
beyond the ghostly trees.

And just when it felt

like it would last forever,
the stars fell down from the sky.
They left us blinded, breathless and bare,
don't think I've ever felt this alive.

For just a glimpse
is all we had,
and all we ever will.
Yet somehow,
I have lost my mind,
for in that glimpse,
time stood still.

And so it goes,
the star and me,
she'll take me beyond this galaxy.

For aren't we all, just glimpses in the sky?
One moment we shine, the next we die.

22. Shooting Star // Discomfort

This piece is about someone for whom I had developed limerence and I had to work really hard for over 2 years to work my way out of it.

Saw my first *shooting star* with you,

it disappeared with the blink of an eye,
just like you did
and I don't know why.
I'd ask, but you'd just lie.

You walk away every day,
leaving behind an empty space
that I try to fill with rationality,
because I want some clarity
that you deny me
and I don't know why.
I'd ask, but you'd just lie.

We lie on separate beds,
readings books in silence.
I hear your calming breath,
wondering if you hear mine as well.

It's so comfortable, yet so unnerving
to be in this room in which we once lay
side by side, throughout the night,
your arms around me, you felt so far away,
I had so much to say
but kept quiet in fright,
as you held me tight. Why?
I'd ask, but you'd just lie.

Getting high in the balcony
2 A M, just you and me.
Going on a chatting spree
as constellations lined the sky
and I, trying to catch shooting stars,
got lost in their sight,
hours and hours passed us by.

Now those hours feel heavy upon me
as I wake up to another day,
where I know you'll walk away
and I'll have nothing to say.

Because, I've said it all,
and it's just pushed you further away.
So now I hold my peace,
trying to find some within me,
hoping it'll set me free
from all of this *misery.*

I've lost you, I know that now,
I won't ask you to stay
like all the times I did before,
cause now I'm too afraid.

I can't bear another no,
I'm really trying to let you go.
Feel free to drop by, anytime you like.
Maybe you'll be back for this T-shirt you've
left behind,
it's lying on my bed, I love your smell,
I'm guilty for soaking in the scent of you,
I'm tempted to try it on too.
But I won't.
Why'd you leave it here to dry?
I'd ask, but you'd just lie.

Seems like I can't do anything right.
You're telling me I'm wrong all the time.
Whatever I do just turns you off.

You're angry, it makes me want to cry.
You look at me with burdened eyes
and I don't know why.
I'd ask, but you'd just lie.

Feels like everything you say
is just to hurt me.
You've not said anything nice to me in weeks.
Lately, everything is my fault it seems.
I don't know what's bothering you,
but you're taking it out on me.
Please don't honey, just let it be.
Just let me be in my *misery.*
Walk away, if that's what makes you happy.
I don't want to cause you any discomfort,
I care too much for that to happen.
Someday you might turn up
to my room with Irish coffee,
on your own, and ask me if I want to get high
and maybe watch a movie
that you think is funny,
and we could catch shooting stars, from my balcony,
just as we did, back when we were free from
all of this longing, guilt and agony.

And maybe then, I'll ask you why,
did you have to leave me so many times?

And maybe then, you'll look into my eyes,
begin *from the start* and tell me why.

And on that night,
the *shine* in your eyes,
will end all of our lies.

23. From The Start

This, as you would find, is a rare piece on optimism.

I never know

When to let go
I never know
If I should at all
I never know
If I should even try
For all of my trying
There is no denying
Has only ever torn us apart

I never know
Why we couldn't be
When what we had
Is all we'll ever need
And I never know

If it was real
When we said our goodbyes
And held back our cries
And hoped it would set us free.

Come back
Come back and *haunt* me
Quit hiding your heart
Cause if it feels like
Our song's a bit broken
Well darling, let's play it from the start.

I never know
When to let go
But honey I,
Never meant you harm
Maybe I'm
Learning how to love
And I'm just hoping, yes I'm just hoping
That it won't tear us apart

Come back
Come back and haunt me
Just quit hiding your heart
And if you feel like
Our song's a bit broken
Well darling, let's play it from the start.

Have you ever wondered
Why it hasn't gone our way
So many hours, wished away on *shooting stars*,
when there was so much to say.

So come back
Come back and haunt me
Just quit breaking my heart
And if you feel like
Our loves a bit shaken
Well darling, I'll meet you at start.
And never grow apart
I'll meet you at the start,
Once again will give you my heart.

24. My Sea Haunts Me

This piece is from the point of view of a beach dog who is in love with the ocean.

The sea is mild today,

her rough edges
smoothed since last night.
My *scent* in the sand
doesn't pass me by.

I can't see my worries,
waves gush over them.
Sounding so *subtle*, so *sweet,*
glistening *silver* sheen
sing of stories swimming underneath.

My pals lost in slumber
dream of this very moment
as we live dreamy lives

sans hunger pangs,
my senses feed on this sky.

And never did the wind
touch me ever so gently,
that I wake up in a *climax,*
bathe in a melting horizon,
salt seeping into cracks

of my fur so fawn,
they mistake me for the sand
and I don't mind,
I'm one with the ocean,
I'm one of her kind.

She is a beauty,
flaunting her turquoise,
foamy in all the right places.
Blackest yet warm.
Even in the dark,
she steals all the gazes.

She is mild today
her roughness
haunts me.
But now, she has reclaimed me.
We'll begin *from the start*, for

now *she has my heart.*

25. Subtle September

This piece is about a moment of calm amidst a raging storm of heartbreak.

Why does September always disappear?

Ever so slightly, makes its presence known.
For years I didn't exist in September,
the rain bled into the fog of winter.

This time though, I feel it,
I think I quite enjoy September.
Maybe because it'll soon be too cold
for solitary slumber
and I'll ache for you,
and that's so harsh, so apparent,
that now I quite enjoy the
subtly of September.

I think I might stay here
for a year,
when the yearning is manageable
and my mind is somewhat at ease.
When I miss you, but barely enough
for it to be bothersome,
when I seek my own company.
In here is where I'll be,
I'll let myself be in September,
it's a *sweet* kind of free.

Desire runs high in August,
I cried along with the clouds.
Behold the lust of December,
the *haunting* loneliness of wintery dusks.
Oh won't you let me hide
in the subtly of September,
where I'm enough for me?

Won't you slip away
from my memory
and into your own September,

where you are you and I am me.

No pain, no regret, no yearning.

September, my dear
is just an *escape* fantasy.

26. Escape Of February

This too is another rare piece of optimism and the cozy feeling of being inside your blanket on a cold winter morning and how the temperature of the insides of the blanket perfectly match that of your body, almost being an extension of your body.

It's been a good February,
the chill lasted till the very end.
All the desires, of sitting around the fire,
have been fulfilled, the winters did amend.

It's a good Sunday, striking up a chord.
The cold air fresh and tense
and legs snuggled into comforters,
comfort finds you in abundance.

You hold on, you dive in deep,
loving the last few days of heaven,

for winters never last as long as they should,
leaving behind memories forsaken.

It's cold *tonight*, let's dance in silence.
The world outside a pleasant still.
Find a friend and sway onto
a cascading platoon of memory *hill*.

You hold on, you dive in deep,
loving the last few days of heaven,
for winters never last as long as they should,
leaving behind memories forsaken.

Come closer, hold onto me,
this warmth is where I want to be.
For its going to end soon,
this wintery *escape*, my epiphany.

You hold on, you dive in deep,
loving the last few days of heaven.
For winters never last as long as they should,
leaving behind memories forsaken.

Come closer, hold onto me,
this warmth is where I want to be.
For its going to end soon,
this wintery escape, my epiphany.

Hold on, pull them close,
subtle moments of embrace,
for winters end far too soon,
the rest you must now face.

So honey, hold onto me,
this love is just what I need.
For its going to end too soon,
this wintery escape, my epiphany.

27. Slow Down Tonight

This piece is for anyone who has faced a rough day and deserves to know that they are enough.

You don't have to be
anything tonight,
sink into your pillow,
all troubles out of sight.
You're lost in the future
or the what could-have-beens,
but this moment right now,
will make it alright.

Life's been funny,
often at your expense
and you've laughed along
all the time.
But once in a while
the joke gets old

and the sorrow, can't *escape*
your smile.

And that's okay,
We've had those days.
We have all, somehow, *survived.*

Yes you may say,
you've had better days,
but even the worst ones,
you have survived.
All that you have been,
all that you will be,
is all that you are,
tonight.

Just let go
of what next and what ifs.
Drink in the *thrill*
of being alive.

Slow down,
you're doing fine,
you don't have to be
anything, tonight.

28. Survive

This one is about a little ephemeral thing called life.

A faint *scent* grips,
setting nerves free,
she hovers high above,
far away from me.
I see her raging on,
this sight will never shift,
yet it's only life,
it's over before we know it.

So much to do,
so much to miss,
some linger on,
some traverse the *beyond.*
Yet all we have is this,
a sight that never shifts,
life will pass you by,

I hope you can *survive*,
yet it's over before you know it.

Say it when you can,
for words may leave you forever.
Can't waste a chance now,
for now has become never.

This fever you can't shake,
tighter than your mother's embrace.
I know how it feels
to leave a lover without grace.
So I pray to *escape* it forever,
before now becomes never.

So much we've felt *tonight,*
and little we remember,
shut ourselves from it all,
wishing we were never born.
All we have is this,
a sight that never shifts,
this life is all there ever was,
it's over before we know it.

29. Beyond

This piece is fictional. Make what you will of it.

Through the open fields,
across the narrow roads,
there once lived *a man,*
you might have been told.

He slept for days on,
held onto his horse,
together they wandered
far from all remorse.

Look at them go,
beyond the highest peak,
into the sunny wonders
of a world unsold.
Untouched by emotion,

painted in time,
but you cannot *escape,*
the devils of your mind.

He tries and he tries
but he cannot let go.
He cries and he cries,
his screams, they echo
and fill these fields
with utter remorse,
as he rides his horse
into a story untold.

I'm tired and so are you.
Simpler times, they remind
of thriving lives and hopes that *survive.*

We take these narrow roads,
we catch onto him,
he cries no more,
and now we begin.

Our screams
float upon the breeze,
the ground splits open
underneath,
and down and down

we all go.
Our stories untold,
we begin to unfold.

Take my hand,
ahead lie rocky roads.
The journey has begun,
we can't go back no more.

Across the ebbing streams,
we discover our dreams,
with the man who sleeps
beyond the open fields.

30. A Man

This piece is about an old man sleeping by the roadside and the sight of him shattered my heart. This one's for him.

The clouds are calm tonight,

prancing through the horizon,
their reflection though speeding up
in the waves raging on in sight.

They shield the moonlight,
never absolutely,
glimpses of stars breaking through
years of unseen time,

and *a man* walks past,
worn out and broken by life,
he longs for some company,
says it might be his last.

Settles down on the *Gangetic* edge,
dangling above the *muddy* waters,
we can’t touch the sky,
our hearts have lost courage.

Strangers in silence
comfortably losing touch,
his voice is never heard
as he sings of his innocence.

A calm seeding the air,
waves leave the clouds behind,
taking along their reflections,
who won the race? He cannot say.

He doesn't care for the end,
he just wants to begin.

The winds will carry on
his troubles,
as they travel to the *beyond,*
long after he is gone.

31. Gangetic Muddy Waters

This piece was written when I saw the Hooghly river from a plane, flying into Kolkata. It made me wonder about the secrets held within the river currents and silts. Ancient waters.

And so it disappears
into a blurred chaos,
will we dive in again
and out of our past?
Who knows,
what the muddy waters behold,
sedimentary sorrows,
a man and his pharaohs?

Dip in but don't drown,
as we often do.
Sail across the shores
in awe of the mystical *blue.*

Keep repeating the mantra
that is *unknown.*

Breathe in, don't breathe out,
this you ought to do.
Navigate with caution
these cerebral hues.

While repeating the mantra
that is unknown.

And so it begins,
voyage of the river.
Can we surrender,
that which we hold dear?

For who knows,
what the current brings,
sedimentary sorrows
nonsensical things?

32. Unknown

This piece was also written on an airplane ride wherein I was looking outside the window, wondering what if we took off into space.

Layers upon layers

floating through
the horizon so *blue,*
reaching out to the *sun,*

building the sky
for your benefit and mine,
clouding our vision,
blocking out the sun.

Where do they come from?
Where will they go?
Stacking up like memories
of *old muddy* reminiscences,

never the same,
they float away.

Lift us up,
rid us of this weight
we've been carrying for ages,
we're waking up but we're not awake,
we'll come *undone.*
Where clouds don't hide the sun,
we can learn to live as one.

Layering our minds,
clarity running low,
we need to go,
ascend into the unknown.

Floating over yourself, *out of body,*
you can be free forever.
What do you chose?
Body or soul?
Wake up or exist in the unknown?

Lift us up, set us free.
Can I be one with me?
I'll find another world.
You'll come undone.
We will walk the sun.

Nothing we can't become.

33. Waking Up But Not Awake

This is perhaps, one of the most challenging pieces I have written. It is about a teenager who dies of rabies on a hospital bed and neither me nor my co-interns could do anything about it.

It's one of those days,
I'm waking up to an *unknown haze*
for the fifth time today.
Mom has been calling,
don't know what to say.

Rain drops glistening
on my car's rear shield,
like million diamonds
trying to talk to me.

But I don't know what to say.

I'm waking up
for the fifth time today.

It's one of those days,
my TV serotonin fazed.
I can't shake off his face,
the boy who gasped for a breath,
and died in front of me yesterday.

I speed on
through a blinding hail
storm, asking myself,
“Will I make it home today?”

His mother's craze,
crying for his life, in my arms
and I didn't know what to say.

Some never awake
and lie *dead* forever.
Yet here I am,
waking up,
for the fifth time, today.

34. Dead // Climax

This piece is inspired by a movie called 'Climax' and is about the uncertainty of life and of the living.

Living is a collective impossibility.

Death is an extraordinary experience.
5 minutes are enough to dream up a lifetime,
that's how relative time is.

You kill yourself in your dream
and live on to watch yourself die,
as you come *out of your body*
and look for a place to hide.

But you can't escape yourself,
you'll rebirth into another you,
a sub-personality you thought you had killed,
only to realize, it had already killed you.

You *wake up* from your death,
as if the endless sleep wasn't all that endless,
it only ends when the dream does,
but another day then, must begin.

And so you live through 24 more hours,
even though you're dead as can be,
peel off your skin, just to cover yourself in it in,
you can't hide from the demons within.

Your birth wasn't your fault,
but your death shall certainly be.
After all, living is a collective impossibility.
Death cannot come for free.

It might be an extraordinary experience,
but you are just so ordinary
that even in death, you don't make a difference,
your existence doesn't matter, you see.

Still we dream up a life in 5 minutes
and 80 years later, your last words will be -
"*Time* is relative, 5 minutes of life is all I ever had
because my life, never had time for me."

35. Lost In Time

This piece is a search for one's inner child.

Look at me,

how deep is your gaze?
Can you see your foes
dancing across my face?

Do you see
a dream floating by,
drowning in the tears
welled up in my eyes?

Do you see yourself in me,
or are you so hard to find?

Reach out and grab yourself,
hold on tight.
A slip of hand, a change of mind

and we are forever lost in *time.*

Look at me
searching through a *haze*,
for a reason that would explain,
why we can't *escape* this phase.

Do you see
a child running by?
You can’t catch up to
what you've lost to time.

He runs further away,
turns around and smiles,
and you *realize*, you've lost
what's yours, I've lost what's mine.

Do you remember him,
or is he so hard to find?

Run up to your *past,*
hold on tight.
It's a *climactic* ride back to the future,
and we are forever lost in time.

36. Past High

This one is about seeing someone beyond the façade of 'adulthood'.

I met you in your low vibe,

fell in love with your *past* high,
took me a while to *realize*
that we're searching for the same guy.

You're not what you used to be,
even though I never met him
I know, he is the one you seek,
even though you want to forget him.

Is it something that you fear
that keeps you away from me?
Or are you just running away
from who you used to be.

Cause I don't want to run anymore
beside you, even though I want to be
in your gravity,
I just want to go for a walk at dawn,
discuss dubstep, maybe meditate,
as we let go of our collective hate.

I'm so tired of chasing you,
while you chase yourself too.
I'm leaving behind a trail of
everything I need to get back to

myself, so here I am, *slowing down,*
let me catch a breath,
please don't turn around
as I watch you head into
a *haze* of forgotten dues
and debts that you owe yourself
from a time when you were true.

I saw a *glimpse* of you when we first met,
the real you, and I had no regret
that I fell for him, but now I do.

Because baby, he's not you.

It was a tiny glimpse,

lasted a day or two
but enough for me to know
that you're going to get through
to him, bring him back,
breathe him in, and when you do,
don't let him go, just hold onto
your vibe from before
we met, and maybe then
I'll meet you again, *lost in time,*
for the first time,
like meeting an *old friend.*
And maybe then
you'll see me too.
See me too like I see you.

And maybe then,
we'll begin again
And maybe then,
we'll begin again.

37. Old Friend

This piece is a true story that took place at the aforementioned 'Spot' on the lake.

He said, as I took his hand

"It's just *skin and bones*"
And though the truth was so,
yet it was so much more.

Tracing my fingertips,
he took me *back in time.*
It was simple, it was fine,
now, it's just you and I.

The water hits our *walls,*
gushing sounds underneath,
moving in waves, circling in time,
now it's just, *you and me.*

He feels he is moving
and the water has no pace.

I see him take off
into his wildest dreams.
My skin warm, his warmer still,
now it's just, *you and me.*

“I see a *child* lost in your *past”*
His words end my *lies.*
Water in my eyes now,
he has found me, I realize.

Come on then,
we've been set free.
Parts of you in me,
until whole of me is you.
Dear *old friend*, now it's just *you and me.*

38. Me And You

This piece is about trying to be friends with your lover.

Beyond *music*, beyond words,
there is a set of *lies*
that lie beneath this
grey sky.

Beyond us
there is a happy life,
if we ever try to seize it,
it expires.

So tell me then,
is it worth a try?
Cause everything we know
has always been a lie.

Leaves of grass,

never ending ever bending
fools
of time that's passed,
and moments that stuck
in me and you.

Beyond trust,
there is haunting sight.
We should never try to look it
in the eye.

Beyond love,
there is a sacred hide.
If we ever try to feel it,
we die.

So tell me then,
is worth a try?
When everything we want
is always hard to find.

Leaves of *grass,*
never ending ever bending
fools
of time that's passed,
and moments that stuck
in me and you.

In me and you
there's something new
there's something unknown.
Never seen,
never heard,
never done before.

And if I say
it ends today,
it ends where it begins.
And when it does,
it ends in us,
it ends only within
Old friends.

Me and you.
Me and you.

39. Music // His Song

Partly fictional, partly true, this one is a recollection of a personal memory.

The music sways away
under my skin
as I sit here
searching

for answers;
I haven't moved,
I'm staring straight into
memories of *me and you.*

Playing right across the window,
they meddle with my mind,
tear it down and sew it up,
send me spiralling in time.

And then I hear
a whisper in the cold,
lips white as ice,
we were scared, yet bold.

We faced the night,
I kissed your *bones,*
you screamed my name,
now I won't die alone.

Then why is the window,
playing tricks on me?
I look into my eyes,
but it's you I see.

I still can't move
or shake off your *scent,*
you never leave
and I can't find you when

I'm searching for answers,
you just lead me on;
The music is mellow,
and *your song* is *gone.*

40. Gone

This one is about unhealthy attachment patterns.

Don’t go, come here,
fill my voids.
You won't go all the way
but you will try,
because you know
that I can fill yours,
and even though it's far from complete,
but, it's just enough

to keep us going
hard at each other.
We fail and we fall
in love with the clutter.

I need you
just for a while,

before I find
a better lover,
who makes the voids
feel not so empty
and that's the *high*
we chase all our lives.

We satisfy our
childhood cuts,
love how it feels to heal
and call it being in love.
I'm nobody's lover,
no one can be mine.
All we want is a *rest*
from chasing ourselves *back in time.*

This is how it goes,
we know it, we live it
we *sing* it, and give it
up, when the healing declines.

Never stop filling in
the voids we can't fathom,
the depths of them all
we fear to imagine.

Let's fall in love

and go hard at each other,
till I fail and you fall
in *love* with another.

41. Love Misery

This one is a cry for help and the only one who can help you out of the situation is the one that placed you in it. It's a paradoxical death wish.

I can't believe I've let you down,

I'm only trying to stay away,
and if someone can turn this around,
then I'd be happy if it *plays* out that way.

Because it's been 9 months
since you went away,
I broke your trust and
things weren't the same.
And every little replay
has led me to stay
in the *shadow*,
of our love misery.

Honey you’re *gone*; why did I ever let you go?
I'm *dancing* alone, you're here no more.
Can't find nobody who talks like you,
even you don't talk like you did before.
Did I ever love you so?
Or was it *Stockholm Syndrome*?

It's been 9 months
since you went away.
I fell out of love
and I wasn't okay.
And every photograph
has led me to stay
in the shadow
of our love misery.

Why can't I see,
you won't be with me?
How do I set myself free?

When all is done
you'll be the one,
the one that'll set me free.

And for that I love you
like the day when we first met,
I'm navigating through this regret.

I'm wiser now, than when I left you,
you're wiser still to ever let me again.

But if you remember me for me,
then lead me out
of this love misery.

42. Stockholm Syndrome

This is fictional yet heavily inspired by some unmet need of being dominated and of being controlled.

See the sunshine

over this barren land,
I fell in *love* in Israel.
Rough as the desert storm,
there lived a man,
lured me in like the devil.

And I could see that
he was crazy,
with a gun on his back,
as he walked up the tracks,
thinking of a hundred ways to
blow up a Cadilac.
And I believe
that's when he attacked,

I had nowhere to run,
not that I even tried,
I had fallen in love
with his crazy eyes.

Loving you, it isn't easy.
Things to do, we got no time to *play.*
Come on and let me go.

Want to get down and get so dirty,
but you don't ever want to ride with me,
oh won't you let me go.

All of this town
seems to know
that you've been playing with my broken soul.
You're so good to me
when I'm wearing a blindfold.
Oh no, you'll never let me go.

Loving you, it isn't easy.
Things to do, we got no time to play.
Come on and let me go.

Want to get down and get so dirty,
but you don't ever want to ride with me,
oh won't you let me go.

Loving you, they say, it's a disease.
Misery ties me up *in your gravity.*
Come on and let me go.

Want to get down and get so dirty,
but you don't ever want to ride with me,
oh won't you let me go?

43. In Your Gravity

This one is yet another true story that happened not so long ago.

I'm sitting outside your door
in *Stockholm,* I don't know what to say.
I know you don't want to see,
the regret on my face,

or hear it in my voice
when I *apologize.*

Just sitting at your door,
failing to convey
the agony I feel
when I see your face,

or hear your *voice,*
but I don't have a *choice.*

I just need to be
within your gravity
and feel like I belong here.
So calm in your gravity,
I could die here
in peace.

You're lying on your bed,
I picture your breathing.
Can I lie next to you?
Guess I'm just deceiving

myself, you don't want me there.
In fact, you want me nowhere,
yet here I am, sitting outside
your door, on the stairs.

I apologize,
I did have a choice
to go the other way.
I could have made you stay.

I drown in my *regret.*
I hope you don't forget
me, for I just want to be
within your gravity.

When I'm in your gravity,
does mine make you feel me?

44. Voice Call

This begs the question of hurting the one you love or loving the one you hurt.

I would call

but then what's the point?
You don't want to talk
and all my thoughts are disjointed.

But I want to call,
just to hear you say
that I'm hurting you
and that I should stay away.
I might just get a ringer
going on and on forever.
Nothing new, this I'm used to,
lonely nights bleed into lonely days.

But then if, oh my god,

you do want to talk,
and you pick up and say,
“Hi”,
I swear I'll melt away,
my mind's going to clear up,
I’ll push through this heartache,
I'll say "Do you want to meet up?
I'm coming *within your gravity* in 3 days."

So do you think I should call?
Do you think you'll be okay?
Hearing my voice shake,
reminds you of your heartbreak
and I know I shouldn't call,
because I know you are not okay
and I can't hear you say ‘Hi’,
your sweet voice will make my heart break.

And I miss you now and all day.
And I miss you through it all babe.
I just miss you till the dawn breaks,
so won't you please just hear me say,

"I miss you now and all day,
I miss you through it all babe,
I miss you till the dawn breaks,
I just that hope you are okay."

45. Lonely Night

This one is a reminiscence.

As you watch your hands shiver,

a chill runs down the spine,
fingers trace *silhouettes*
of memories left behind.

And you sway in the wind,
the mist, your company,
a far away land
sees your lover shine.

So glide in and tap out,
keep up with the rhythm,
so much you've given,
you wish you had forgotten.

A nightly *voice* speaks to you,

as your breathe clouds your eyes,
the mind wanders far off,
to a land where your lover shines.

Farewell to whispers,
giving chills down the spine,
lips brushing against the *skin,*
now seem of another *lifetime.*
So glide in and tap out,
keep up with the rhythm,
so much you've given,
you wish you had forgotten.

Just glide in and tap out,
scream if you will.
You watch your hands shiver,
your spine curves to the *chill.*

46. Silhouette

This one is dedicated to the ones who intoxicate. Spoiler alert, it does not numb the pain, it just makes your already emotionally hard hit body now also physically and chemically hard hit.

Don't do drugs.

Seeking a laugh or two,
a face of familiar pain,
a friend who is just as sane,
covering the endless gloom.

Every smell and each *taste*
of sinful delights,
every touch, every kiss,
spent in vain, in search for a sight.

A sight that promises

calm and bliss that shall
fulfill this craze
of staying alive.

Will you ever touch, just to feel
the warmth that creeps underneath,
or will you always waste every breathe
trying to deceive yourself?

See thoughts run wild,
give up the pill
that might ease the guilt
of not being what we should be.

Visions stir up your unhinged mind.
Screams of surrender must make a sound.
Reach out and come alive,
your spirit knows no bound.

But just as you wait and watch
a smile so sad on such a lovely thing,
you realize this shall go on,
that there is no escaping.

You trip, you intoxicate,
you kill yourself, as the *smoke rises* higher.
Visions of *lonely nights,* sights unseen,

your senses arrested, and forever shall be.
Wake up. Pass out. It's all but a *dream.*

47. Hope Leaves

This one is based on a vivid memory of attending an Opeth concert.

Calm yourself,

wet eyes, *goodbye.*
Cold, twisted mind,
sinks in too deep,
search, but you cannot find.

The *smoke rises* up,
and with it goes
everything left behind.
Never to rise again
from fires that kindled kind.

Touch and *taste* the *silhouette,*
it looks like you.
Withered by *hopes*

kept, some broken too.

You can see me rising,
I'm floating over you.
I gave you all my love,
you gave me all your doom.

Hurry,
dry *lips.*
Cold, *blue skin.*
I'm in your blood stream,
your defences were thin.

The smoke rises up
and with it comes
everything that was left behind, *goodbye.*
Never to settle in vain,
this will linger on through time.

Touch and taste the ashes,
you look like them.
Weightless and worthless,
growing from a common stem.

Do you see me rising?
I'm hovering over you.
I've got you in my arms,

you're choking in my tomb.

48. Goodbye

This one is about acceptance.

Some nights,

there is nothing left,
as if you didn't make an effort at all.
Wiped out of existence,
a spectator of their altered reality.
Watching them forget everything you once shared,
with 'friends' who don't get them,
in a town you both held sacred,
singing along to *Hope Leaves,*
unaware of how it will, one day.
One night when you'll realize
there's nothing left.

The *afternoons* are hard,
never felt the time pass by
so slowly.

When I had you, it flew by in an instant,
years in minutes and days in seconds,
only to leave me stranded now for hours,
in memories of you.

Each morning, I own up to my mistakes.
It's never enough.
I wish you success, it's never enough.
I apologize, it's never enough.
It never will be.
So I must learn from you,
how to let go of me.

It doesn't matter anymore,
what I do is of no consequence to you.

I don't exist in your reality,
your wall is all I can see.

I try to hate you, I fail.
I fail to hate myself too.

I love you.
I'm trying to love myself too.

I need you more than ever,
but you won't ever know

and so, I must go.
There is nothing left of me in you.

49. Your Wall

This one is when you feel completely helpless and powerless and you wish to scream out to your lover but you are screaming into an empty room.

You put up a wall
to save yourself
from my insanity.
So what do I do
with all of this build up
against your wall?
All my *regret,*
it ricochets back at me,
it tears through my heart
like a possessed drilling machine.
I let out a scream,
scream after scream,
till all the *blood* has left me
and I collapse into your wall,
can you hear me fall?

You put up a wall
to save yourself from my apology.
You believe it's a lie,
I don't blame you.
I'd doubt myself too.
Now all of this build up
against your wall,
is wrapping itself around me,
I can't even let out a scream.
I can't breathe in this sea of
apologies, I need to rest, but I'm drowning.
I go down, and down and down,
till all the air has left me.
I collapse into your wall,
can you hear me fall?

You put up a wall
to save yourself from my love,
it was too much.
I wish it wasn't so,
what do I do
with all of this love
beating against your wall?
It's dying, it won't come back to me.
You are the only place
it wants to be.

It keeps crashing and crashing
and crashing, but you won't let it through.
It's dying, against this wall of you.

It can't take down your wall.
I know you can hear it fall,
you just say *goodbye* to it's call
and then do *nothing at all.*

50. Rest

This one is an attempt to ask for forgiveness and peace.
It also takes you back to the start.

Ever since I left

that little old feeling,
my days of laughter
have left me too.
And here I am,
breathing in the *blues.*

Never saw this coming,
didn't see it go,
like remains of a love
I can feel no more.
Every now and then,
I hear a chair creaking
that reminds me of sleeping
with you in the cold.

Just you and I,
warm in the cold.

I speak with the *gods*
to right my wrongs,
will this ever lift off my chest?
Sweet nothings
fill up my hours,
will I ever lie in rest?

Ever since I left
that little old feeling,
my days of anger
have left me too.
Here I stand,
breathing in the blues.

Never saw this coming,
can't watch it go.
Reminds me of a love
I can feel no more.
But every now and then,
I hear the leaves rustle,
that remind me of walking
with you, up the *hill.*

Just you and I,

and the world so still.

I pray to the gods
to right *our* wrongs,
will this ever lift off our chest?
Sweet nothings
filling our souls,
as we wonder if we'll ever *rest.*

Printed by Libri Plureos GmbH in Hamburg, Germany

9 789369 532148